MY FIRST BIRD BOOK

Text and illustrations by S. D. Schindler

Learning Ladders/New York

The author wishes to donate the proceeds from this book to the National Audubon Society, Inc.

Published in the United States by Random House, Inc., New York, and
simultaneously in Canada by Random House of Canada Limited, Toronto.
ISBN: 0-394-84613-3   Manufactured in the United States of America   1 2 3 4 5 6 7 8 9 0

Do you know what these animals are? Yes! They're all birds. What makes a bird a bird? If you think of these four things, then you've got a bird:

Feathers. All birds are covered with feathers. No other animal has them.
Wings. All birds have wings, and most of them use their wings to fly. Flying is what birds do best.
Beaks. All birds have beaks (or bills) instead of lips and teeth.
Eggs. All birds lay eggs in nests they build for that purpose. All baby birds come from eggs.

Just look at some of the many different shapes and sizes birds come in! Some are brightly colored and others are drab. Some are tiny while others are tall. Their tails and claws, beaks and wings vary greatly.

We can classify birds according to what they look like and where and how they live. Just as people do, each kind of bird, or **species,** has its own likes and dislikes. Each bird chooses a place to live and hunt for its favorite foods. We call that place its **habitat.**

A habitat is a place where plants and animals form a community. The type of land, or **terrain,** the amount of rainfall, and the temperature all determine the kinds of plants and animals that form that habitat.

Almost anywhere we find ourselves, we are in a kind of habitat. Let's visit some different habitats and discover the birds living there.

The City

Skyscrapers and subways, trucks and cars, sidewalks and streets and people, people, people—what an odd habitat the city is! Yet it is home to some kinds of birds. Birds living in the city depend almost entirely on people for their food and even for their shelter. They eat the food people throw away or offer them. And they use buildings for nesting and **roosting**, or sleeping.

You see here the three most common kinds of city birds. The large gray bird is a pigeon. Pigeons like to roost in tall buildings. Large flocks visit parks, where people feed them bread crumbs, watch them strut and waddle, and listen to their gentle *coo-cooing*.

The dark bird with the speckled feathers is a starling. It also likes to feed on tidbits in the park. In the evening, starlings gather in huge numbers to roost on buildings. Starlings are a screechy lot. A group of them can be heard from blocks away.

The smallest city bird is the house sparrow. That's the male with the black bib. Sparrows travel in small flocks, *cheep-cheeping* as they hop about looking for seeds or crumbs. They live in other habitats as well, such as the suburbs and the countryside.

The Suburbs

Halfway between the city and the country, the suburbs are where people live in houses surrounded by gardens and lawns. Like people, many birds find the suburbs an ideal habitat. There are lots of things to eat—worms and insects, fruit and seeds. And lots of places to build nests—in trees or bushes and also on a drainspout or other nook or cranny of a house or garage.

See the grayish-blue-and-white bird on the tree trunk? That's a nuthatch. He hunts for insects in the bark.

The bright red bird with the head crest is a cardinal. Cardinals have a lovely song and a mild manner. They hunt mostly for fruit and seeds.

The bird with the orange breast is a robin. Robins love to eat worms.

The little striped bird with the rosy breast is a purple finch. Finches like to nest under the eaves of houses or in ivy growing on a wall.

The tiny bird with the black cap is a chickadee. Chickadees are very acrobatic flyers and have a merry song that goes like this: *chick-a-dee-DEE-DEE!* Can you make a noise like a chickadee?

The pretty blue bird with the crest is a blue jay. Blue jays are smart and noisy and very curious birds. They will eat almost anything they can find or catch, even another bird's eggs!

Fields, Meadows, and Grasslands

Here we are in the wide open spaces, where natural grasslands or cleared pasture lands provide a wonderful habitat for certain birds.

The large bird is a ring-necked pheasant. It spends most of its time on the ground, pecking about for seeds. It is especially fond of corn and wheat. When startled, a pheasant will erupt into flight, clucking loudly.

The bird with the bright yellow breast is a western meadowlark. From a fence post or power line, he sings his sweet, cheerful song. Farmers like meadowlarks because they eat the caterpillars that attack crops. Unfortunately, many larks are killed by pesticides sprayed by the very farmers they help.

The round-bodied bird with the patterned feathers and its young in tow is a bobwhite quail. Quails and many other kinds of birds in this habitat hatch their eggs in nests on the ground. Within hours of hatching, the babies are up and running behind their parents in search of food.

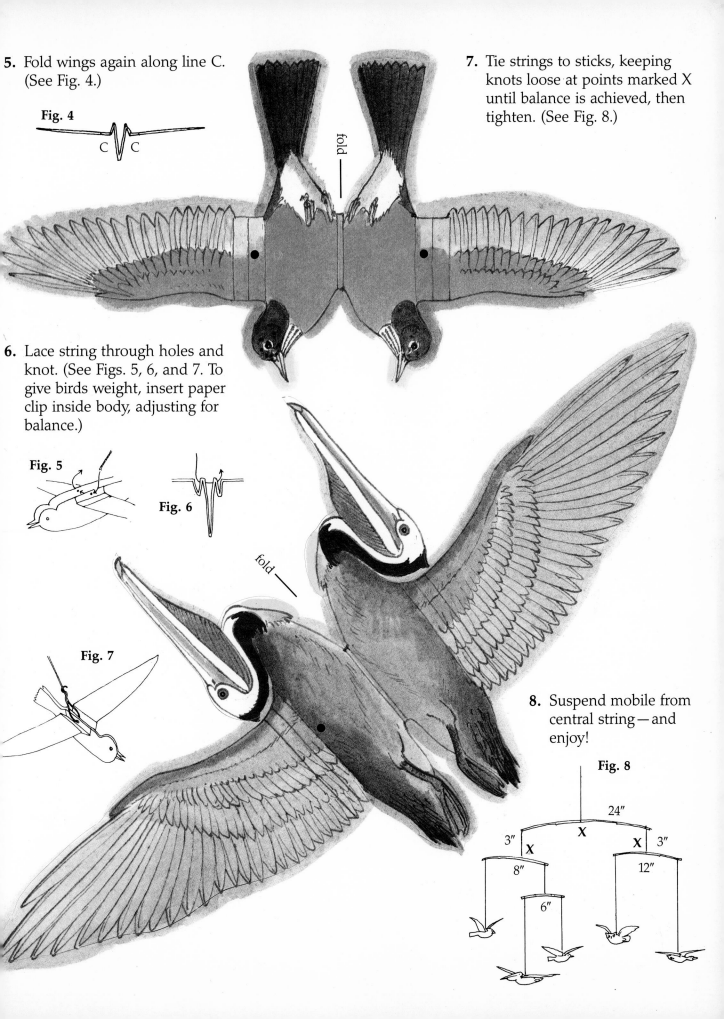

5. Fold wings again along line C. (See Fig. 4.)

Fig. 4

C C

fold

7. Tie strings to sticks, keeping knots loose at points marked X until balance is achieved, then tighten. (See Fig. 8.)

6. Lace string through holes and knot. (See Figs. 5, 6, and 7. To give birds weight, insert paper clip inside body, adjusting for balance.)

Fig. 5

Fig. 6

Fig. 7

fold

8. Suspend mobile from central string—and enjoy!

Fig. 8

24"

X

3" X

X 3"

8"

12"

6"

Forest Trees

Forests are very complex communities, and birds have found many ways to fit in. Some birds spend all their time in the treetops, while others run about on the ground. Many spend only their summers in northern forests and fly to warmer places down south for the winters. Many forest birds are small and difficult to see among all the leaves, but they have beautiful songs that can be heard from some distance.

Do you see the little brown bird hopping down the tree trunk? That's a brown creeper. He eats insects and their eggs, hidden in the bark crevices.

The bird with its beak open, singing, is a hermit thrush. His is a most melodious song. Hermit thrushes like cool woods with running water.

The pretty gray-and-black bird is a catbird. Catbirds can mimic other birds' songs as well as the sounds of animals, like cats.

The little gray-and-white bird with the bright eye is the solitary vireo. Vireos love caterpillars—and this vireo is just about to catch himself a juicy one.

The black-and-white bird with the red head patch is a hairy woodpecker. Hairy woodpeckers find grubs by listening for them within a tree trunk. Then they peck a hole and pull the grub out with their tongues.

The bright red-and-black bird is a scarlet tanager. Tanagers live high up in the treetops, where they hunt for insects and fruit.

The Forest Floor

Doesn't that large bird look familiar? It ought to. It's a turkey. Turkeys spend the day foraging on the ground for seeds, nuts, fruit, insects, and even frogs and snakes. At night, turkeys roost in groups high up in tall trees.

The little bird with a worm in its bill is an ovenbird. Ovenbirds spend all their time on the forest floor, where they also build their dome-shaped nests out of twigs and lichens.

Can you see the whippoorwill? Whippoorwills' feathers help them hide among dead leaves on the ground. They fly about at night, catching insects in their large, gaping mouths.

The bird with the big eyes and feathery ears is a screech owl. Screech owls hunt at night for rodents, large insects, and the occasional bat.

Wetlands

Many birds are attracted to the watery areas around lakes, ponds, rivers, and marshes because of the vast variety of foods to be found there.

The tall, graceful bird is a blue heron. Its long legs and neck and pointed beak help it catch fish, frogs, and crayfish in the shallow water.

The bird diving for fish is the common loon. Loons are very strong swimmers but very shy, so don't try to get too close to one. Enjoy it from afar, especially the sound of its "loony" call.

The bird paddling along with its young is a mallard duck. The most common form of duck, you will probably be able to see one in the wetlands near you.

Perching on the reed stem is a red-winged blackbird. You'll find redwings in marshy areas thick with cattails, singing their song, which goes like this: *ok-a-LEE!*

The Seashore

Many birds make their homes in the dunes, cliffs, and beaches of coastal areas.

See that bird with the large bill and throat pouch? That's a pelican. When pelicans dive after fish, they open their mouths and suck in up to three gallons of water. Then they squeeze out the water through their nearly closed bills and swallow the fish that remain trapped in the pouch.

The dark bird below the pelican is a cormorant. Cormorants are also divers. Their feathers aren't as water-repellent as those of some other water birds, and so after they have dived, they need to stand with their wings outstretched to allow their waterlogged feathers to dry in the sun and breeze.

Those soaring birds are sea gulls. Their plaintive cries and graceful flight are familiar to everyone who has ever visited the seaside. They will eat almost any kind of food and are very clever scroungers. They'll even steal fish from pelicans or cormorants.

Those little birds running along the water's edge are sand-pipers. They're hunting for tiny shellfish in the sand. Sandpipers are fun to watch because they run and fly in formation, like dancers.

The Desert

The driest habitat of all, the desert is also a land of harsh extremes—very hot during the day and very cold at night. Animals and plants that make their home here in the desert must be very good at dealing with these conditions.

See the bird running after the lizard? That's a roadrunner, and it is fast enough on foot to run down its prey.

The bird standing on the mound is a burrowing owl. If you approached it, it would not fly off. It would simply dive into the hole. These owls sometimes share their burrows with prairie dogs or rattlesnakes. Burrowing owls eat any small desert animal they can catch, especially rodents.

The bird poking its head out of the cactus is a gila woodpecker, and that cactus is its home. When it moves on to another cactus, other birds and animals will come along and take over its nest. One kind of bird that often inherits the woodpecker's nest is eyeing him from the thornbush right now. That's the cactus wren.

Get to Know the Birds Near You

Early morning and evening are the times when birds are most active. Sit in one spot and wait for them or go walking in search of them. But be very quiet. Birds are timid and easily frightened. Keep a record of your bird-watching: your very own bird book. A small notebook will do. Try to draw pictures of them. Print their names underneath. A grownup will help you with the spelling.

Pine Cone Feeder: Fill a pine cone with peanut butter or suet. Then roll it in birdseed or sunflower seeds. Tie a string to the bottom and hang it from a bush or branch. Make sure you hang it high enough so that other critters can't get at it.

Milk Carton Feeder: Ask a grownup to cut a large, square hole in the side of a cardboard gallon milk carton. Tie a string to it, fill it with seed, and hang it high.